AF091934

# Time Is, Was, Will Be

Saint Julian Press
Poetry

# Time Is, Was, Will Be
## By Matt Bialer

SAINT JULIAN PRESS
HOUSTON

Published by
SAINT JULIAN PRESS, Inc.
2053 Cortlandt, Suite 200
Houston, Texas 77008
COPYRIGHT © 2026
TWO THOUSAND AND TWENTY-SIX
©Matt Bialer

Paperback ISBN-13: 978-1-955194-50-1
Library of Congress Control Number: 2026930699

Cover Art Credit: Matt Bialer
Cover Design: Smythtype Design

www.saintjulianpress.com

*For Isabel (Izzy) Bialer Lapidus*

*I am always so proud of you. You never cease to amaze me.
I love you.*

Time Is, Was, Will Be

Time is too slow for those who Wait,
Too swift for those who Fear,
Too long for those who Grieve,
Too short for those who Rejoice;
But for those who Love, Time is not.

—from "Time is" by Henry Van Dyke

## Time Is, Was, Will Be

### I.

Today is Sunday
November 5th
Four and one-half years
To the day
After my wife
Lenora
Died of breast cancer

She died
On May 5th

Also a Sunday

Sometimes
It feels like
Long ago
That she was alive

Long ago

Other times
It feels like
Just a few months

Just a few months

But as
More time goes by

It's feeling like
Long ago
That she was alive

Long ago

She was
Last with us
54 months ago

54 months

I used to count
How many Sundays
I was out
From her death

It was
Like swimming
Further and further
Out in the endless ocean

The endless ocean

The land
I was leaving behind
Her life

Land was
Her being alive
Our 30 plus years together

Land was
Our first date
At Café Dante
On MacDougal Street
In Greenwich Village
New York City

She played footsie
With me
Under the table

I had
Never had
A woman
Be so bold
With me
On a first date

Not one
I admired so much
And was attracted to

Even though
It was a first date
I had known her
Since 6th grade
When I had
A crush on her

She had long dark hair
Wore a blue ski jacket
With lots of patches
Of mountains she skied

Mountains she conquered

And the chair lift tags
She collected
On her jacket's zipper
She loved
Collecting the tags

Just as
Later in life
She collected
The badges
She wore
From the many conferences
She attended
As a well-known civil rights lawyer

Long ago

Land was
Her being alive
Our 30 plus years together

Friday
April 19th, 2019
Her last Passover seder
Just days
Before she died

I knew
She wanted
The comfort
Of a nice Passover meal
Her favorite holiday

But I was
Too tired
To cook it
From scratch

Too tired
Too scared

I got everything
Pre-prepared:
Brisket
String beans
Casseroles
Charoset

Swimming
Further and further
Out in the endless ocean

I hand fed her
Her last food
Spoonfuls of
Noosa raspberry yogurt

They were
Giving out free samples
On the street
And so I took one
And tried it
And loved it

So I started buying
Noosa yogurt
And she loved it too

Noosa

Creamy Noosa
Made from milk
From Colorado
Was one of
Our little secrets
A shared love

Raspberry
Blueberry
Pumpkin

I hand fed her
Her last food
Spoonfuls
Of Noosa raspberry yogurt

Spoonfuls

Until a nurse
Told me
Not to try
And feed her

"Food doesn't matter anymore"

I couldn't believe
I was hearing that

Couldn't believe

Food doesn't matter anymore

Further and further
Out in the endless ocean

The endless ocean

The land
I was leaving behind

I used to count
How many haircuts
I got
Since she died

How many haircuts?

Until I stopped
Counting

Stopped counting

But it's been
28 haircuts

Even though
I stopped counting

Stopped counting

How many haircuts?

Long ago
That she was alive

Our daughter Izzy
Is now 21
And a senior
At Barnard College

She was 16
When her mother died
A junior in high school

From her perspective
The land
Of Lenora's life

The land
Of having
A mother

Is a long, long time ago

On the other side
Of the world

The other side
Of the world

And today
This Sunday
Is Daylight Savings Time

The clock
Moves backward
In time

We gain an hour
A precious hour

Today is 25 hours
Instead of 24

I try to think
Good thoughts
That Izzy is coming home
This evening
For two nights
From Barnard

That it is now
The Fall
And my girlfriend
Of 3 and ½ years
Mary
Loves the Fall
Just like me

Among many things
We have in common

Many things

And this Tuesday
SLAY will have dinner
At Mary's apartment
On the Upper East Side
Of Manhattan
For a late group celebration
Of Mary's birthday

SLAY

A 4-way-text thread
Between Mary
Me
Izzy
And Mary's daughter Samantha
Who is Izzy's age

We post funny memes
Texts
Videos
Make plans

We had to cancel
The celebration
On Mary's actual birthday
Because Samantha
Tested positive
For Covid

We had to cancel

Swimming
Further and further
Out in the endless ocean

The endless ocean

The land
I was leaving behind

## II.

I'm excited
To see Izzy
Tonight

And for SLAY

To celebrate
Mary's birthday
On Tuesday evening

I am tasked
With buying the cake

Mary wants one
With yellow sponge
And chocolate frosting
Which is exactly
What I would want

Figures

I am excited
About stuff
But I have
To get through
The rest of the day

The rest of the day

Daylight Savings Time

Figures the longest day
Of the year is today

25 hours

Spring forward
Fall back

And I keep reading
About the wars
In the Middle East
And Ukraine

So much
Pointless death

And I spend
So much time
Struggling with
This one death

The one
That hit me
The hardest
In my life

Pointless death

One death

25 hours

Daylight Savings Time
DST
The practice
Of advancing clocks
Typically by one hour
During summer months
So that darkness falls
At a later clock time

The typical implementation
Is to set clocks forward
By one hour
In either late winter
Or early spring
"Spring forward"

And to set clocks back
By one hour
In either the fall
"Fall back"
To return
To standard time
As a result

There is one 23-hour day
In early spring
And one 25-hour day
In the middle
Of autumn

Which is today

I thought
There was talk
Of getting rid
Of the whole thing?

We're not
A nation
Of farmers anymore
Who needed
The extra light

Probably candlelight
At the time

When Izzy
Was focused
On astrophysics
She once told me
That time is not real

Time is not real

Is 4 and ½ years
Since she died real?

Is our 30 plus years?

Is time real?

I didn't think
4 and ½ years
Would affect me
The way 4 years did

But it has

It has

Real or not

Real or not

Sometimes
I feel
So helpless

I just
Never know
When grief
Will spring
On me

A jolt

A surprise attack

What most people
Don't know

Don't understand

That it's always
Apparent
Always
In my life

It's turned me
Into a freak

A mutant

It's a sea monster

A leviathan

Swimming
Further and further
Out in the endless ocean

The endless ocean

The land
I was leaving behind

I am
Always in conflict

Like I'm
Trying to withstand
A brutal invasion

A war within myself

A bombed-out hospital
Like I see on the news
And social media

The disintegration
Of my own infrastructure

I have been invaded

Invaded

I don't want
To post
About Lenora
On this milestone day
That's not
Really a milestone

A 25-hour day

Time is not real

I used to count
How many haircuts
I got
Since she died

How many haircuts?

Until I stopped
Counting

Stopped counting

But it's been
28 haircuts

Even though
I stopped counting

Stopped counting

How many haircuts?

Long ago
That she was alive

I see
On my Facebook memories
My posts
On this day

A year ago
Two years ago
Three years ago
Four years ago

And I feel guilty
Leaving behind
The land of my life

So I decide
To post
If just
For Izzy's sake:

I choose a few photos
Of her
And me and her
And the three of us:

"4 and ½ years ago
We lost Lenora
It was
A very early Sunday morning
May 5, 2019

It will always be
'That Day'

I miss her
All of the time
But I'm also
Making big decisions
On moving forward
With my life
It took me awhile
But I accept
The fact
That she's not here anymore
That she won't
Get to attend
Izzy's graduation
From Barnard College
In the spring

We will never wander
The streets
Of Paris again

The mundanity
Of having breakfast
On a Sunday morning

So many adventures
Just stopped

But Izzy and I
Are each
On other journeys "

I text Mary
That I posted
She's well aware
Of what today is

She writes back:
"Beautiful post"

I tell Mary
That she's a part
Of the "big decisions"
In the post

That I will move
To the Upper East Side
Of Manhattan
To be physically closer
To her
That Mary is
"My other journeys"

But she
Already knows that

Already knows that

So many adventures
Just stopped

"That day"

Izzy texts me
That she's on the train
The Amtrak
From Saratoga Springs
Where her boyfriend
Seamus
Goes to school

She's on four-day break
And she spent
The first two
With him

On the train
Going to Penn Station
Izzy texts me:
"Can we go to
Krupa tonight?"

Krupa Grocery

Our go-to
Neighborhood restaurant

Izzy's comfort food
When she comes home

I used
To go there
With Lenora
Most Fridays
Every week

Most Fridays

After she died
I was afraid
To go

It took me awhile
To reclaim it
Take it back
Like conquered land

Conquered by death
And grief

Is time real?

It feels real
Always there
Inexorably moving forward

Time has flow
Runs like a river

Time has direction
Always advances

Time has order:
One thing
After another

Time has duration
A quantifiable period
Between events

Time has
A privileged present

Only now is real

Time seems to be
The universal background
Through which all events proceed

Such that order
Can be sequenced
And durations measured

The question is
Whether these features
Are actually realities
Of the physical world

Or artificial constructs
Of the human mind

Time may not be
What time seems

Izzy would tell me
It's an artificial construct

An artificial construct

I get a private response
About my post on Facebook
From someone
Who worked
With Lenora
At the ACLU
The American Civil Liberties Union

"Am delighted to see
On Facebook that
You and Izzy
Seem to be thriving
And keeping Lenora alive
In your hearts

You know better
Than me
But I would think
She would be
Happy to see this

As I say
She showed us
How to live"

How to live
Because she
Always was
A fighter
And would lose herself
In her work
And family
Even though
She was ill

How to live

And how to die

I am touched
By the message
But it also
Makes me
A little sad

For a moment
I feel guilty
That I can
Be happy

Guilty

Would she
Be happy
For me
That I'm
With Mary?

I guess so

But I'm not
Always sure

She could
Be a jealous person

And sometimes
I feel weird
That because people see
Photos of Mary and me
Looking happy together
That they assume
That I am always happy
Because they want
To believe that

I'm better now

They don't have
To worry

It's like
I took some miracle drug
And I'm cured
Of my grief

Cured

I'm off their hands

But I also think
It doesn't matter

Doesn't matter

And I am happy
With Mary

It was
Like swimming
Further and further
Out in the endless ocean

The endless ocean

The land
I was leaving behind
Her life

Land was
Her being alive
Our 30 plus years together

Before it gets dark
On this 25-hour day
I take a walk
To Prospect Park
Where Izzy and I
Had a tulip tree
Planted in Lenora's memory

Planted
2 and ½ years ago

25-hour day

Time is not real

The tree is
Where I go
To reflect on her
Like today

I know others
Come here too

It's gotten taller
And its leaves
Are turning golden

It gives me
Some comfort
Some solace
That there's
A tree
Something living
In the park
She so loved

Just blocks
From our house

That night
Izzy and I
Go to Krupa

I am so glad
I took back Krupa

Took back Krupa

It was
Conquered by death
And grief

But I mounted
A counter offensive

Took it back

Just like
I took back
Noosa yogurt

I couldn't even
Look at it
For awhile

Creamy Noosa
Made from milk
From Colorado
Was one of
Our little secrets
A shared love

Raspberry
Blue berry
Pumpkin

I hand fed her
Her last food
Spoonfuls
Of Noosa raspberry yogurt

Spoonfuls

Until a nurse
Told me
Not to try
And feed her

"Food doesn't matter anymore"

I couldn't believe
I was hearing that

Couldn't believe

Food doesn't matter anymore

Further and further
Out in the endless ocean

The endless ocean

It feels great
To be with my daughter
She orders
Her usual avocado toast
With prosciutto
And I order
A shrimp burger

We're both
Well aware
Of what this day is
This 25-hour day

I ask Izzy
About time
Not being real

Is time real?

She talks about
A four-dimensional
Space-time structure
Where time
Is like space
In that every event
Has its own coordinates
Or address
In space-time

Time is senseless

All points
Equally "real"
So that future
And past
Are no less real
Than the present

So are we being misled
By our human perspectives?

Is our sense
That time flows
Or passes
And has a necessary direction
False?

Are we giving
False importance
To the present moment?

I don't know

But I do know
That this moment
Being reunited
With Izzy is real

Our daughter Izzy
Is now 21
And a senior
At Barnard College

She was 16
When her mother died
A junior in high school

From her perspective
The land
Of Lenora's life

The land
Of having
A mother

Is a long, long time ago

On the other side
Of the world

The other side
Of the world

Time is not real

## III.

On Tuesday afternoon
I walk into
Regina Bakery
In my neighborhood
In Brooklyn
To choose
A birthday cake
For Mary

The celebration
Is tonight

Yesterday
I walked
Into Regina
And scoped out
The choices

I actually
Walked into
Another bakery
As well
But I didn't like
The shapes
Of the cakes
In Butterly Bakeshop
They're too narrow
And tall

And if
I don't like them
The chances are
Mary won't either

A few days ago
I took the F train
A few stops
From where I live
In Park Slope, Brooklyn
To Carroll Gardens
Not too far
From where Lenora
And I
Used to live
Decades ago

Decades

Court Street
Has a lot of
Old World Italian bakeries

But I stick
To my own neighborhood
That has its own
Old-fashioned bakery

The daughter
Of the owner
Of Regina
Tells me
That they do have cakes
With yellow sponge interiors
Topped by
Chocolate frosting

Perfect

Exactly what
Mary wants

And that's
What matters

That's
What matters

Regina Bakery

Been in
The same family
For over 50 years

These days
It's in
A slightly smaller version
Of its original spot

A cozy
And warm space
Feels like
It's been the same
For decades
Certainly since
I moved
Into the neighborhood
In 1996

The large window
Often foggy
This time of year
From the oven heat
In contrast
To the crisp
Fall weather
Outside

Decorated
With thank you cards
From local kids
Who love
Their desserts

The glass display counter
Is filled with color:
Classic Italian rainbow cookies
Golden cannoli
Fluffy eclairs

More cookies:
The Cookie Monster
Green turtles
Purple dinosaurs

I choose
The cake
That I want

And while
The daughter
Of the owner
Is boxing it

I look
At an old
Black and white photograph
On the wall
Protected by
A clear plastic bag
With some flour on it

It's former
New York City mayor
Ed Koch
In the old location
Holding a cake
In a box

Ed Koch

Charismatic and funny
Mayor of New York
A long time ago

From 1978 to 1989

In the bakery
A long, long time ago
Like it could have
Been today

Could have
Been today

She was 16
When her mother died
A junior in high school

From her perspective
The land
Of Lenora's life

The land
Of having
A mother

Is a long, long time ago

On the other side
Of the world

The other side
Of the world

Ed Koch
A long, long time ago
Through a foggy window

Time is not real

Later
I'm holding the cake
And some of Izzy's bags
As we take
The subway
From Brooklyn
All the way
Up to the Upper East Side
Of Manhattan
Where Mary lives

After dinner
And birthday cake
Izzy will
Take an Uber
Back up
To Barnard

On the subway
Izzy and I
Talk more
About time

Is time real?

Time is, was, will be?

We can portray
Our reality
As either
A three-dimensional place
Where stuff happens
Over time
Or as a four-dimensional place
Where nothing happens

Nothing happens

And if
It really is
The second picture
Then change
Really is
An illusion

An illusion

Because there's nothing
That's changing

It's just all there

Past
Present
Future

Time is, was, will be

So life
Is like a movie
And space time
Is like the DVD

There's nothing
About the DVD itself
That is changing
In any way
Even though
There's all this drama
Unfolding
In the movie

We have the illusion
At any given moment
That the past
Already happened
And the future
Doesn't yet exist

And that things
Are changing

But all
We're aware of
Are our brain states
Right now

Right now

I tell Mary
That she's a part
Of the "big decisions"
In the post

That I will move
To the Upper East Side
Of Manhattan
To be physically closer
To her
That Mary is
"My other journeys"

But she
Already knows that

Already knows that

So many adventures
Just stopped

"That day"

A 25-hour day

Time is not real

I used to count
How many haircuts
I got
Since she died

How many haircuts?

Until I stopped
Counting

Stopped counting

But it's been
28 haircuts

Even though
I stopped counting

Stopped counting

How many haircuts?

Long ago
That she was alive

Mary serves us
A wonderful dinner
Of chicken pot pies
Caprese sticks
Salads
And grape leaves

Before we have
Birthday cake
Izzy discussed
A documentary series
She's been watching
On Netflix:
HOW TO CHANGE YOUR MIND

Based on a book
About psychedelic therapy
By Michael Pollan
And also
Hosted by him

A wide-ranging look
At psychedelic therapy
In particular
It focuses
On four substances:

LSD

Mescaline

MDMA aka Ecstasy
Or Molly

And psilocybin
The active ingredient
In magic mushrooms

And the ways
In which
They are being used
To treat patients
With maladies
Including post-traumatic stress disorder
Addiction
Depression
Anxiety
And obsessive-compulsive disorder

Michael Pollan
In his late 60s
Tall and bald
Fit as a swimmer:
"At this age
Sometimes you need
To be shaken out
Of your grooves
We have to think
About these substances
In a very clear-eyed way
And throw out
The inherited thinking
Thinking about it
And ask
'What is this good for?'"

The filmmakers
Had said:
"We didn't want
To fall into the trap
Of using psychedelic visual tropes:

Wild colors
Rainbow streaks
Morphing images

We wanted
To keep the visual style
More personal
Intimate
And experiential
We wanted people
Watching this series
Who have not had
Their own psychedelic experience
To be able
To relate to the visuals"

Classic Italian rainbow cookies

The Cookie Monster
Green turtles
Purple dinosaurs

From her perspective
The land
Of Lenora's life

The land
Of having
A mother

Is a long, long time ago

On the other side
Of the world

The other side
Of the world

Ed Koch
A long, long time ago
Through a foggy window

Time is not real

Izzy says
The series
Has really opened up
Her mind
To the huge potential
Of psychedelics
To really
Help people
Get over mental
And emotional obstacles

Like grief

And sometimes
I feel weird
That because people see
Photos of Mary and me
Looking happy together
That they assume
That I am always happy
Because they want
To believe that

I'm better now

They don't have
To worry

It's like
I took some miracle drug
And I'm cured
Of my grief

Cured

I'm off their hands

But I also think
It doesn't matter

Doesn't matter

And I am happy
With Mary

It was
Like swimming
Further and further
Out in the endless ocean

The endless ocean

The land
I was leaving behind
Her life

Land was
Her being alive
Our 30 plus years together

I remember
People telling me
I should
Smoke weed
To help me
Get over my grief

Smoke weed

But I had stopped
A long time ago
And now
Was no time
To start again

I was afraid
Of being paranoid
Which is
The last thing
I needed

No
It wasn't me

And I have
My doubts
That psychedelics
Would be either

I took LSD
A few times
And that was
Back in 10th grade

The last time
I took it
I called
A friend
Named Rich
On a rotary phone
To tell him
Where we should meet
And he said:
"You just called me
We were

On the phone
For 20 minutes
Yes I know
Where we're meeting"

I thought
He was kidding

But he wasn't

He wasn't

I had lost
Like an hour

Unaccounted for

Nowhere
In time

My own personal
"Spring forward"

Daylight Savings Time

An hour
Lost in time

It took me awhile
To reclaim it
Take it back
Like conquered land

Conquered by death
And grief

Is time real?

It feels real
Always there
Inexorably moving forward

Time has flow
Runs like a river

Time has direction
Always advances

Time has order:
One thing
After another

Time has duration
A quantifiable period
Between events

Time has
A privileged present

Only now is real

I put the candles
In the cake
And Samantha lights them

Mary blows out
The candles
And we all sing
"Happy Birthday"

When the cake
Is cut
Mary says to me:
"You got me
The cake I wanted"

I reply:
"Of course I did
I listen to you"

Izzy drew
A beautiful card
For Mary
Which also says
Things like
How Mary has become
Such an important part
Of her life
And how grateful she's been
That Mary's been around
For Izzy's entire Barnard journey
And how much

Of a super mom Mary is
To Samantha
And how she's
A loyal, consistent partner
To me
And a reliable confidant
To Izzy
About life
And career
And everything

I'm so glad
That Izzy
Feels this way

It's so important

For the moment
Time is everywhere
And nowhere

I am so happy

Ed Koch
A long, long time ago
Through a foggy window

Time is not real

Time has
A privileged present

Only now is real

Time seems to be
The universal background
Through which all events proceed

Time has flow
Runs like a river

Time is, was, will be

ABOUT THE AUTHOR: Matt Bialer is the author of over a dozen poetry collections, including *ALWAYS SAY GOODNIGHT* (KYSO Flash, 2020), *MAZE* (Finishing Line Press, 2021), *VIEW-MASTER LAND* (Finishing Line Press, 2023), *MATRIX* (Saint Julian Press, 2023), and *FANTASTIC VOYAGE* (Stalking Horse Press, 2025). His poems have appeared in many print and online journals, including *Le Zaporogue, Green Mountains Review, Gobbet, Forklift Ohio,* and *H_NGM_N*. In addition, Matt is an acclaimed black-and-white street photographer whose work has been widely exhibited. Some of his images are in the permanent collections of The Brooklyn Museum, The Museum of the City of New York, and The New York Public Library. He is also an accomplished watercolor landscape painter with work in many private collections.

www.ingramcontent.com/pod-product-compliance
Lightning Source LLC
LaVergne TN
LVHW090038080526
838202LV00046B/3871